OneNote  Beginners:

Microsoft OneNote Computer Program Tutorial Guide For Better Time Management, Organization and Productivity

By

Joseph Joyner

Table of Contents

OneNote For Beginners: Microsoft OneNote Computer Program Tutorial Guide For Better Time Management, Organization and Productivity

By Joseph Joyner

First Published, 2015

Printed in the United States of America

Introduction

One of the best programs from Microsoft is OneNote and unfortunately, this is one among those programs that are being ignored. If you have neglected this program for some reason before, then you should definitely give a second thought about Microsoft OneNote. It is now present everywhere like on Chrome, Android, Mac OS and definitely on Windows. The project managers and business analysts should pay more attention towards this program.

Chapter 1. Basics of OneNote

What Actually is Microsoft Onenote?

Are you looking for something that can help you in organizing everything at one place like your information, notes and also with some additional features? Then here is the answer for your search and it is Microsoft OneNote. Along with organizing your information and notes in one place, you will also be able to enjoy a few more additional benefits like you will be able to find whatever you want in just a few seconds and also you will be able to share the information with others and work effectively from anywhere.

What Forms of Data Can Be Stored and Organized in Onenote?

You will be able to organize and store

Pictures

Text

Audio files and

Video files

To Whom Is OneNote Best Suited?

Do you meet a lot of people during your working hours, regarding work or projects? Are you handling too many projects? Do you attend a lot of meetings, without enough gap? Then you are the right person who should start using OneNote right away. You will be able to place all the information at one place and that is going to look tidy and neat as well. You will not have to spend too much of time, even for searching the notes that you have saved in OneNote. You will even be able to search the text that is present in the images. All the information or notes that you are saving are saved in the cloud and hence you will be able to access it with ease and also share it with ease.

There may be many similar applications available in the market nowadays, but they all do not match with the features that this application can provide you like the audio recording facility, hand writing tool, typing tool and the best is searching tool that you have in OneNote.

To start working with OneNote, you will just have to install that on your device where you want to use it and then login into it with the Microsoft credentials. If you are not having Microsoft credentials, then you can create one and then login and get started with it.

Chapter 2. The Best Way to Get Started with OneNote

1.) You can use this OneNote in preparing your shopping lists. There are many people who always forget why did they go to a supermarket and what was the item that they wanted to buy there. They will not be able to recollect it until and unless, they make a call to their home and find out. Have you ever been in that kind of situation? Then this OneNote is just for you. You can use it for preparing your shopping list and you can easily complete your job at the supermarket. It is not necessary that your device has to be Windows supporting device to have OneNote in it. It is supported by a few more platforms and hence you can use it in your Android, Mac OS or iOS as well.

2.) You can manage all your favorite recipes in your OneNote. Yes, when you see any picture of a recipe or the complete recipe given, then you can make use of the camera to click the pictures of it and add to the recipe labeled section of your Notebook.

3.) You can use OneNote for recording any session. Yes, you will be able record anything that you wish to.

This is very useful for people who belong to the field of music or something like that. Like if you are a musician and you want to have all your composed music at one place, then this is the app for you.

4.) You can make your interview taking session very simple. If you are going to take an interview, then you can record all the question in advance and play the questions. You will have to make use of the pause and play button in between.

5.) There are many people who will be looking for an apt tool or app that can convert the image into text. Yes, conversion of an image into text can be really tough, and sometimes you will have many errors after conversion, but you are not going to face any problem when you have OneNote on your computer or phone device. You can easily scan the image and the image is converted into text in just a few minutes. This is just amazing and many people are going to love this feature of OneNote. You can even search for text in images and that is just an awesome feature of OneNote.

6.) This is one of the best tools for implementing the concept of GTD. You can get the things done with ease.

If you are planning to print something like an email or any other document and then save in your physical folders for further requirement. Then you can do it without having to store it physically. You can select the document or email and give print option, but then you will have to save it the required folder just like you do with physical folders.

7.) Sharing of documents or anything is just in real time and it is instant as well. It is not going to take a lot time for you to share any document with anyone. When you and your colleague were supposed to give a presentation and if you are late or stuck in a traffic jam, then you can share it using OneNote and then your colleague is going to take care of the rest. Only if that data is something related to a project and you want all the team members of the project to read, then you can place in the folder which they are having access.

8.) Make your note taking experience much better. When you are in a meeting, then you can switch on the OneNote on your laptop and then you can tag all the important points in it. By doing this way, you will be able to recognize all the important points easily and then you can share it with everyone.

Chapter 3. Formatting Notes Using OneNote

You will not find any kind of difficulty in preparing your notes with the help of OneNote because it is as simple as writing something on a piece of paper. But with the help of same OneNote, you will be able to format the notes as well. You can easily move or copy the text or images from one place of the page to another place or you can even move or copy them to another page.

What all can be done?

1.) Taking notes on pages

2.) Moving text on the same page

3.) Adding Space

4.) New page creation

5.) Pages order can be changed as per requirement

6.) Note saving

7.) Date and Time Insertion

8.) different kinds of lists can be created

9.) Editing the hyperlinks

10.) Screen clipping can be done

11.) Table creation

Chapter 4. Securing Files on OneNote

Whether it is personal or official information that you are storing on the OneNote app, security of the data is very important. You may sometimes wish to share a few folders with your friends or colleague, but definitely not the entire Note Book.

How to apply password protection?

You should first select that folder or the section, which you want to protect using a password. Then click on the FILE and "password protect this section" has to be selected. Now select "Set Password", and enter the password that you want to set. Next step is to confirm the password and you are done. You can do the same thing whenever you want to change the password.

Normally, you can set password to just a few sections or your notebook or you can set a password to the entire notebook as well. This option of setting the password to each section is making it a more secured option for saving and sharing notes. Even if your entire notebook is copied to another place, no one will be able to access the password protected sections at all.

Chapter 5. Using OneNote on Your Mobile Devices

OneNote is an amazing app and that can be used on Mobile devices also, along with computers and laptops. You don't need a Windows supported mobile device for using it, you can use in other Android devices as well. You may not be able to enjoy all the features that you enjoy on your computers, but there are enough features for your mobiles as well. You will be able to create, edit and share your notes as well. Carrying your mobile device along with you can be easy, while you are not able to carry your laptop along with you.

You can get the app for onenote.com website. You will first have to select the device type and then download it. Once the installation process is done, you will have to login into the app with the Microsoft id credentials. Now, you can create a new notebook or you can even choose to use the existing notebook of your computer. If you want to use the ones that are saved on your computer, then you will first have to save them on the One Drive.

Chapter 6. OneNote And Productivity

One of the best productivity tools that is available along with Microsoft Office Suite is OneNote. You are going to enjoy a lot of benefits by installing this app on your computer or laptop. This app is going to help with better productivity. Here is how it can help in better productivity.

1.) You will be able to capture the screenshot with a lot of ease. You can capture a part of the screen with the help of windows button and S button. You can entire copy the entire screen image to your OneNote or you can choose to crop it and select just a part of it. You don't even have to copy and paste an image that is captured. You can just drag and drop.

2.) Conversion into text from the picture is another important feature that can help in enhancing your productivity. OneNote is going to make use of the OCR system and this is how you will be able to get the best quality output when converted from picture to text. You will just have to right click on the image or picture that you want to convert, and then select Copy text from Picture.

3.) Annotate images is one of the amazing features that are provided by OneNote. Yes, you will be able to annotate with ease and that is not going to affect the original image. Even after you annotate, the original image is going to remain the same and unmodified as well. You can do this using the annotate ink and there is another advantage of this. If you have used this ink for generating handwritten notes in a meeting or any interview, then it is going to be very simple to convert from Ink to text. You should just use one simple command and that is Ink to Text and it is all done.

4.) Creation of any kind of notes is possible with the help of OneNote. You can easily create notes and any types of notes like bullet points, check box, radio buttons, to do list, number lists and many more.

5.) Creation of tables was never so easy like it is now. You can just start the creation of tables by entering the names of the column headers. You can use tab to move to the next column and enter the next header. Once you are done with all, then you can start entering the information that you desired to enter.

6.) You will now be able to carry your special notes and information to wherever you want. You will have to carry some extra file, if you want to take the printouts in a physical form. But if you are saving everything in OneNote, then you will just be carrying the device and if it is your phone, then you are not going to carry any extra weight along with.

7.) You can now easily record the entire meeting conversation if you have some official waiting to know about the meeting. Your higher official may not be able to attend the meeting as they are busy with another meeting or not well. So in that case, you can record the entire meeting conversation in order to show it to your higher official. It will be easy for them to know what exactly happened in the meeting and how to proceed in the next meeting. It can also be regarding an interview as well. You can record the entire interview to show it to the official for taking the final decision about selection. This is very useful if your boss is not available at the time of the interview, but if he wants to take the decision himself.

8.) You will be able share the information at an instance and at the same time you have an option to lock the information that you do not want to share with anyone else. All the information that is present on the OneNote is always safe and you can use it anytime and in the way you want to like sharing it with just a few people in the team and hiding from others.

9.) You can easily embed or link the information from the other office applications into OneNote. You can also sync the to do list and the emails as well. Sent to OneNote is the option that you should use for doing this syncing and linking. You can choose to place this information into any of the existing sections or you can choose a new section.

Chapter 7. Benefits of OneNote App

OneNote is an application which was released in the year 2003 and since then there are many followers for this app. Many people have mentioned that they are unable to manage their tasks without the help of OneNote and they are now surprised that how did they manage till today without such wonderful app. When there are so many people using this, then there must be many benefits of this app. Here is the list of benefits that you can enjoy using OneNote.

1.) One of the best benefits and this is the most common benefits that are talked much when it comes to OneNote. This is a single place you will be able to place all your audios, videos, your image collections, your plans, your ideas and all sorts of research that is done by you. You can keep all the information just like the way you are going to save all the information physically. In fact, this is of the best ways, because you can use it in any kind of device. This is an app from Microsoft, but that does not mean that you will have to use only those devices that support Microsoft. You can use it in Android, Mac OS or iOS as well. So, the selection of the device is completely dependent on you only.

2.) You will not have to struggle with printers and print out organizing process with OneNote. Yes, you are going to become completely digitized with the help of OneNote. There are many experts an businessman who still takes print outs of the very important documents and then mark the important points for further help. They also write some special notes on the margins of the printouts. But for all these people OneNote is a boon and you can do all these without taking any kind of printouts. You will also be able to enjoy much more interesting features as well.

3.) You can make your meetings much more effective than they are till today. Generally, when you are attending any meeting like project meeting, then it is very important for you to take notes of the points that are being discussed in the meeting. This is going to help you in taking the right action according to the requirement. You can have all the information that has happened in the meeting by recording it and then you can share it with those who missed it. Or if the meeting was with the higher officials and you want your juniors to know about the meeting, then this would be the best way to share exactly what has happened in the meeting.

4.) You can share the notes that you have created, with anyone that you wish to. After a meeting with your customer, you want your team to know the exact conversation, then make note of all the points and then you can share those with the team so that they can start working on it. You are going to stay on top in your team if you are able to organize everything well between your team members.

5.) You can make your information more organized by using the tables or spreadsheet option. OneNote is all about organizing the information and you will be able to do it in a much better way if you are using a spreadsheet. Creation of tables is very easy and you will be done just be entering the header details of each column. You can now create the row information when the column header are all ready for you.

Chapter 8. Things to Know About OneNote

There are many interesting that you get to know about OneNote when you are searching online, but do you know that there a few points that you did not know about OneNote. If you want to know, then continue reading...

1.) Is your operating system Windows? Then which version of it are you using? Is it Windows 2010? Then did you anytime notice that OneNote is already present in your computer. Yes, since the 2010 version of Microsoft Windows, the OneNote has been included in it. You can now click on your windows button and check it right away if you have never seen or don't believe this.

2.) The OneNote is the name of the app and it does not mean that you need to have just one note. You can take as many notes as possible for you and that is completely dependent on the space that you have. If you are acting a little smart, then you can store all your notes on the SkyDrive and that is having 7 GB space on the cloud and that is going to be more than enough. If you think that is not going to be sufficient for you, then you can consider buying a 200 GB external device and start storing it.

3.) The entire magic of OneNote is completely based on the 3 R's. You are going to read, write and do arithmetic as well. You can read the read anything that you want to from the notes that you have like the documents that you stored, the documents that you have written or you can read the images that are written using ink. You can also convert the handwritten text and images into text if you are not able to understand them well. You can write whatever you want to write using the hand or you can even use a stylus for writing. You can use markers for highlighting the text or making any kind of notes on the printouts. And finally, when it comes to doing arithmetic operations, then you will be able to calculate it very easily. You will just have to type the entire or write the equation and then press the space bar. You have the answer for any kind of or any complex equation waiting for you. When you read arithmetic operations can be done on the OneNote, then you must not have been much surprised, but what if you are told that it can work calculus? Yes, it can solve all levels of Calculus equations as well.

4.) Did you want time have a look at the type of papers that are available at the OneNote. If you are feeling that using just a normal plain paper is not enough for you, then you can check the styles of papers available at this OneNote and you will be surprised by the number of paper styles that you get to see and use. You will not be able to find so many varieties even at the local stationary store. Not just the local stationary store, but you will not find it anywhere else.

5.) You have help for OneNote and that help is always available for free. Although using this simple Microsoft app does not require any kind of help, you still an option to take help from them and you should make the best use of it when you are able to get it for free.

6.) There are many shortcuts available with OneNote and it is going to be very interesting and easy for you if you are able to earn all of them with a lot of care. OneNote is already making your job easy and if you are learning the shortcuts, then you are going to make it much simpler.

Chapter 9. Keyboard Shortcuts

Here are keyboard shortcuts for making the working on OneNote simple.

Alt   N   File insertion on the current page

Alt   N   File insertion on the current page as printout

Alt Shift P   Current page's document printouts would be shown or hidden

Alt   N   Insertion of a image from the selected file

Alt   S   Insertion of a image from the camera or scanner

       S   Insertion of screen clipping

Alt Shift   D   current date insertion

Alt Shift   F   current time and date insertion

Alt Shift   T   current time insertion

Shift Enter   Insertion of a line break

Alt = A mathematical equation would be started or the text that you are selecting would be converted into an equation

Alt Tab Creating a table already typed text by adding 2nd column to it

Enter New row creation when reached end of the table

Ctrl Enter New row creation below the current row

Alt Enter Creation of another paragraph in same cell in table.

Alt Ctrl R Creation of column to right of current column in the table.

Alt Ctrl E Creation of column to left of current column in the table.

Alt Ctrl Enter Creating of row above current one in the table

Alt Ctrl Delete Deletion of the current row in the table which is empty

There are many more such interesting shortcut keys for using with OneNote and you will be surprised to know that this simple OneNote can be made much more simple and you can enjoy them as well.

Chapter 10. Tips and Tricks For Effective Work

1.) One simple trick or tip that is very important is you will have to learn the shortcuts. This point has been discussed earlier and learning them will even reduce the time that you need for searching and opening menus to do something the text or image that you are working on. While checking for menus or other stuff, you may miss out some interesting points that you want to miss like missing a few very important points.

2.) You have an option for changing the screen size and you should make use of this point. You will have many things in and around the page where you are taking notes, these things that are around may distract you and hence you can maximize the size, so that you will have just the screen that you needed and you can make the best use of it.

3.) Using your OneNote along with other Microsoft applications is a very good practice and you should start making use of it.

4.) Searching in the images for text is a very common point and that is known to almost all the OneNote users. OneNote uses the OCR and will be able to identify it very well, the text that you are looking for. But do you know that you can search for text in the audio and video that is recorded. Not many of you are aware of this point, but the fact is this is also possible.

5.) If you are using OneNote in the smart phone or tablets, then it is always good to protect your notes with passwords. Basically, OneNote is not the place for saving any kind of critical information, but sometimes you will have to record a few business meetings, but you are not willing to share with anyone. In that case, this OneNote password will be of great help for you. So, all that you don't wish to share has to be protected by yourself.

Final Words

There are many organizations and other firms which are having the complete license of the Microsoft Office, but not many of them have really tried it at least once. In fact, not many of them are aware that this is also available along with the license for which they have paid. Coming to many individuals, they have installed this Microsoft OneNote in their devices and that was just because it was compatible, but not many of them have actually tried it by themselves. Do not be part of this team who has not tried it yet. If you are having a touch screen device like a smart phone or tablet, then this an app for you and you should definitely try it this time. You are also going to enjoy the fully digitized world of yours using the OneNote App.

Installing this on your device and using it is not at all difficult and if you are still having any questions, then you can check on the Microsoft website for official information. If you are still having many more queries, then you can get in touch with the help support that is available for free. You will get answers for everything in this kind of places.

Individuals and organizations, both are going to enjoy the benefits of this OneNote app, if you are making use of all the features that are valuable with this app. Many features are not aware to many people, like many people who are using Microsoft suit 2010 are not aware about its existence in their PC. Learning and operating it is very simple and you can also take a backup all the old that you may no longer need in your device. You can still get back all that information back into your device whenever you need it.

Thank You Page

I want to personally thank you for reading my book. I hope you found information in this book useful and I would be very grateful if you could leave your honest review about this book. I certainly want to thank you in advance for doing this.

If you have the time, you can check my other books too.